Pride Matters

Pride Matters

EDITED BY

Lorraine A. DarConte

ARIEL BOOKS

**Andrews McMeel
Publishing**

Kansas City

01 02 03 04 05 BIN 10 9 8 7 6 5 4 3 2 1

Library of Congress Cataloging-in-Publication Data

Pride matters : qoutes to inspire your personal best / edited by Lorraine A.
DarConte.
   p. cm.
   "Ariel Books."
   ISBN 0-7407-1883-5 (pbk.)
   1. Success—Quotations, maxims, etc. 2. Motivation
(Psychology)—Quotations, maxims, etc. I. DarConte, Lorraine A.
PN6084.S78 W49 2001
646.7—dc21   2001022656

Design by Susan Hood

ATTENTION: SCHOOLS AND BUSINESSES
Andrews McMeel books are available at quantity discounts with bulk pur-
chase for educational, business, or sales promotional use. For information,
please write to: Special Sales Department, Andrews McMeel Publishing,
4520 Main Street, Kansas City, Missouri 64111.

Contents

Introduction

When you think of the word *pride,* what comes to mind? Winning a medal in the fifty-yard dash in first grade; catching your first fish; high school graduation day; getting your first job; helping your department reach its sales goals; having a baby; holding your grandchild for the first time.

There is no doubt whatsoever that pride is important. If you don't have enough pride, your dreams may go unfulfilled, your goals may be left unreached. If you have too much, the world can quickly become a very lonely place.

It's the *right* kind of pride that matters: the kind that reminds us of the importance of hard work, diligence, and loyalty; that we should always do our best; that learning is a necessity; that we must always try, try, and try again; that there is always room for improvement.

Pride matters. It has always mattered. It is something we need individually and collectively. It is something that must be developed over time. Pride—the right kind—is demanding, humbling, unyielding, exacting, and uncompromising. Gathered in this book are quotations from people from all walks of life who all know how important pride is.

Hold Fast
to Dreams

I always have to dream up there against the stars. If I don't dream I'll make it, I won't even get close.

—*Henry J. Kaiser,*
founder, Kaiser Steel
(1882–1967)

You need to have dreams. Everything starts
with a dream.

>—*Sheila Douty,*
>*Olympic medalist in*
>*softball (b. 1962)*

When I look into the future, it's so bright it
burns my eyes.

>—*Oprah Winfrey,*
>*television talk-show*
>*host, actress (b. 1954)*

Dream lofty dreams, and as you dream, so shall you become. Your vision is the promise of what you shall one day be; your ideal is the prophecy of what you shall at last unveil.

—*James Allen,*
novelist
(1849–1925)

To dream anything that you want to dream, that is the beauty of the human mind. To do anything that you want to do, that is the strength of the human will. To trust yourself, to test your limits, that is the courage to succeed.

—*Bernard Edmonds*

When a man has put a limit on what he can do, he has put a limit on what he can do.

—*Charles M. Schwab,*
CEO, Bethlehem Steel
(1862–1939)

High achievement always takes place in the framework of high expectation.

—*Jack Kinder,*
consultant
(b. 1928)

Cherish your vision and your dreams as they
are the children of your soul; the blueprints of
your ultimate achievements.

—*Napoleon Hill,*
speaker, writer
(1883–1970)

Don't aspire to be like me. Be better. Shoot higher.

> —*Florence Griffith Joyner,*
> *winner of three gold medals*
> *at the 1988 Olympics*
> *(1959–1998)*

My motto—*sans limites.*

> —*Isadora Duncan,*
> *dancer, writer (1877–1927)*

When you reach for the stars, you may not quite get one, but you won't come up with a handful of mud either.

—*Leo Burnett,*
advertising executive,
Leo Burnett Company
(1891–1971)

I have heard it said that the first ingredient of
success—the earliest spark in the dreaming
youth—is this: dream a great dream.

—*John A. Appleman*

It's fun to set goals, and then reset them.

—*Bonnie Blair,*
Olympic gold medalist
in speed skating
(b. 1964)

Somehow I can't believe that there are any heights that can't be scaled by a man who knows the secrets of making dreams come true. This special secret, it seems to me, can be summarized in four Cs. They are curiosity, confidence, courage, and constancy, and the greatest of all is confidence. When you believe in a thing, believe in it all the way, implicitly and unquestionably.

—*Walt Disney,*
film producer, entrepreneur
(1901–1966)

Whatever we believe about ourselves and our ability comes true for us.

> —*Susan L. Taylor,*
> *editor in chief,* Essence
> *(b. 1946)*

It's easy to say "no!" when there's a deeper "yes!" burning inside.

> —*Stephen R. Covey,*
> *writer, cofounder of Franklin*
> *Covey Company*

If you want to succeed you should strike out
on new paths rather than travel the worn paths
of accepted success.

> —*John D. Rockefeller,*
> *industrialist, philanthropist*
> *(1839–1937)*

Nothing happens unless first a dream.

> —*Carl Sandburg,*
> *poet, biographer*
> *(1878–1967)*

Either you have your dreams or you live your dreams. I'm not all that remarkable. I just keep putting one foot in front of the other until I get to where I want to go.

> —*Zoe Koplowitz,*
> *multiple sclerosis sufferer*
> *who finished New York City*
> *Marathon by walking with*
> *two canes (b. 1948)*

Potential: It's all in there. You've just got to work it out.

—*Glenn Van Ekeren,*
speaker

Get involved in everything you've ever dreamed of doing.

—*Marion Jones,*
world champion sprinter
and long jumper
(b. 1975)

Ideals are like stars: you will not succeed in touching them with your hands, but like the seafaring man on the desert of waters, you choose them as your guides, and following them you reach your destiny.

> —*Carl Schurz,*
> *politician, journalist*
> *(1829–1906)*

And our dreams are who we are.

> —*Barbara Sher,*
> *self-help author*

Lord, grant that I may always desire more than I can accomplish.

> —*Michelangelo,*
> *painter*
> *(1475–1564)*

A dream is your creative vision for your life in the future. You must break out of your current comfort zone and become comfortable with the unfamiliar and the unknown.

—*Denis Waitley,*
speaker, writer

To believe in something not yet proved and to
underwrite it with our lives; it is the only way
we can leave the future open.

> —*Lillian Smith,*
> *writer, social critic*
> *(1897–1966)*

A man's dreams are an index to his greatness.

> —*Zadoc Rabinowitz*

We need to give ourselves permission to act out our dreams and visions, not look for more sensations, more phenomena, but live our strongest dreams—even if it takes a lifetime.

—Vijali Hamilton,
sculptor, artist, poet

Dreams come true; without that possibility,
nature would not incite us to have them.

> —*John Updike,*
> *author, critic*
> *(b. 1932)*

Shoot for the moon. Even if you miss it you
will land among the stars.

> —*Les Brown,*
> *motivational speaker,*
> *writer*

When you absolutely have to land that plane, there *will* be a runway—even if you can't see it sometimes.

> —*John Hamm,*
> *managing director of*
> *operations, Internet*
> *Capital Group*

There are so many things that we are capable of, that we could be or do. The potentialities are so great that we never, any of us, are more than one-fourth fulfilled.

—Katherine Anne Porter,
short story writer, novelist
(1890–1980)

To accomplish great things, we must not only act but also dream, not only dream but also believe.

—Anatole France,
writer (1844–1924)

There will always be a Frontier where there is an open mind and a willing hand.

—Charles F. Kettering,
engineer, inventor
(1876–1958)

Success is a journey, not a destination.

>—*Ben Sweetland,*
>*inspirational writer*

Dreams show you that you have the power.

>—*Helen Schucman,*
>*poet (1909–1981)*

What every man needs, regardless of his job or the kind of work he is doing, is a vision of what his place is and may be. He needs an objective and a purpose. He needs a feeling and a belief that he has some worthwhile thing to do. What this is no one can tell him. It must be his own creation.

—*Joseph M. Dodge,*
banker, government official
(1890–1964)

Dream big and dare to fail.

—*Norman D. Vaughan,*
explorer

Your goal should be out of reach, but not out
of sight.

—*Anita DeFrantz,*
Olympic medalist in
rowing (b. 1952)

We've removed the ceiling above our dreams.
There are no more impossible dreams.

> —*Jesse Jackson,*
> *clergyman, civil rights*
> *leader (b. 1941)*

We're all capable of climbing so much higher
than we usually permit ourselves to suppose.

> —*Octavia E. Butler,*
> *science fiction author*
> *(b. 1947)*

You must take personal responsibility. You cannot change the circumstances, the seasons, or the wind, but you can change yourself. That is something you have charge of.

>—*Jim Rohn,*
>*speaker, writer*

Only he who can see the invisible can do the impossible.

>—*Frank Gaines*

The will to win, the desire to succeed, the urge to reach your full potential . . . these are the keys that will unlock the door to personal excellence.

—*Eddie Robinson,*
football coach
(b. 1919)

Are you disappointed, discouraged and discontented with your present level of success? Are you secretly dissatisfied with your present status? Do you want to become a better and more beautiful person than you are today? Would you like to be able to really learn how to be proud of yourself and still not lose genuine humility? Then start dreaming! It's possible! You can become the person you have always wanted to be!

—*Robert H. Schuller,*
author and clergyman
(b. 1926)

Passion and
Enthusiasm

Great dancers are not great because of their technique; they're great because of their passion.

> —*Martha Graham,*
> *founder, Martha Graham*
> *Dance Company*
> *(1894–1991)*

I don't sing a song unless I feel it. The song don't tug at my heart, I pass on it. I have to believe in what I'm doing.

—*Ray Charles,*
singer, songwriter
(b. 1930)

If you're passionate about something, then you should pick up your flag and run with it.

—Bette Midler,
actress, singer, comedian
(b. 1945)

Winning isn't everything, but wanting to win is.

—Vince Lombardi,
football coach
(1913–1970)

We could hardly wait to get up in the morning.

—*Wilbur Wright,*
pioneer in aviation
(1867–1912)

Life loves the liver of it.

—*Maya Angelou,*
author and poet
(b. 1928)

One of the things I learned the hard way was it does not pay to get discouraged. Keeping busy and making optimism a way of life can restore your faith in yourself.

—*Lucille Ball,*
comedian, actress,
head of Desilu Studios
(1911–1989)

Ah, but a man's reach should exceed his grasp—or what's a heaven for?

> —*Robert Browning,*
> *poet (1812–1889)*

Enthusiasm moves the world.

> —*Arthur James Balfour,*
> *British statesman,*
> *philosopher*
> *(1848–1930)*

I believe you have to make your own opportunity. You really have to get going. Get out! Find 'em! Set 'em up! Do 'em!

>—*Diana Ross,*
>*singer, actress*
>*(b. 1944)*

Passion is the trigger of success.

>—*Anonymous*

We have to do the best we can. This is our
sacred human responsibility.

>   *—Albert Einstein,*
>   *physicist (1879–1955)*

Take calculated risks. That is quite different
from being rash.

>   *—George S. Patton,*
>   *U.S. Army general*
>   *(1885–1945)*

Whenever I get to a low point, I go back to the basics. I ask myself, "Why am I doing this?" It comes down to passion.

> —*Lyn St. James,*
> *race-car driver*
> *(b. 1947)*

Quality is a proud and soaring thing.

> —*Jessica Julian*

One can never consent to creep when one feels
an impulse to soar.

—*Helen Keller,*
blind and deaf author,
lecturer (1880–1968)

Developing your own mind and your psyche
will keep you in control of your own reality.

—*Sister Souljah,*
singer (b. 1964)

The worst bankrupt is the man who has lost his enthusiasm. Let a man lose everything in the world but his enthusiasm and he will come through again to success.

—*H. W. Arnold*

Self-esteem isn't everything; it's just that there's nothing without it.

—*Gloria Steinem,*
writer, feminist
(b. 1934)

The main thing is to care. Care very hard, even if it is only a game you are playing.

—*Billie Jean King,*
tennis pro (b. 1943)

The height of your accomplishment will equal
the depth of your convictions.

—*William F. Scolavi*

Success is not the result of spontaneous com-
bustion; you must set yourself on fire first.

—*Reggie Leach,*
hockey player
(b. 1950)

47

The person who does not work for the love of work but only for money is not likely to make money nor to find much fun in life.

> *—Charles M. Schwab,*
> *CEO, Bethlehem Steel*
> *(1862–1939)*

If you follow your bliss, doors will open for
you that wouldn't have opened for anyone else.

—Joseph Campbell,
educator, mythologist
(1904–1987)

Passion is in all great searches and is necessary
to all creative endeavors.

—Eugene W. Smith,
photojournalist
(1918–1978)

49

The pessimist sees the difficulty in every opportunity; the optimist, the opportunity in every difficulty.

> —*Lawrence Pearsall Jacks,*
> *clergyman, writer,*
> *philosopher*
> *(1860–1955)*

You have to be careful about being too careful.

> —*Beryl Pfizer,*
> *writer*

People with passion are incredibly inventive and tenacious individuals. They go way beyond the call of duty and frequently either work on their passion without pay or give more of themselves than their pay warrants.

—Janet O. Hagberg,
writer

When people tell you, "No," just smile and tell them, "Yes, I can."

> —*Julie Foudy,*
> *cocaptain of the U.S.*
> *women's national soccer*
> *team (b. 1971)*

If you risk nothing, then you risk everything.

> —*Geena Davis,*
> *actress (b. 1957)*

To feel valued, to know, even if only once in a while, that you can do a job well is an absolutely marvelous feeling.

—*Barbara Walters,*
television commentator
(b. 1931)

No pessimist ever discovered the secrets of the stars, or sailed to an uncharted land, or opened a new heaven to the human spirit.

> —*Helen Keller,*
> *blind and deaf author,*
> *lecturer (1880–1968)*

I'd rather be a failure at something I love than a success at something I hate.

—*George Burns,*
comedian (1896–1996)

Chase your passion, not your pension.

—*Denis Waitley,*
speaker, writer

It isn't success after all, is it, if it isn't an expression of your deepest energies?

>—*Marilyn French,*
>*author (b. 1929)*

My passions were all gathered together like fingers that made a fist. Drive is considered aggression today; I knew it then as purpose.

>—*Bette Davis,*
>*actress (1908–1989)*

You are embarking on the greatest adventure of your life—to improve your self-image, to create more meaning in your life and in the lives of others. This is your responsibility. Accept it, now!

> —Dr. Maxwell Maltz,
> *cosmetic surgeon,*
> *author (1899–1975)*

Passion is the engagement of our soul with something beyond us, something that helps us put up with or fight against insurmountable odds, even at high risk.

—*Janet O. Hagberg,*
writer

Doing Your Best

I firmly believe that any man's finest hour—this greatest fulfillment to all he holds dear—is that moment when he has worked his heart out in a good cause and lies exhausted on the field of battle.

—*Vince Lombardi,*
football coach
(1913–1970)

A problem is a chance for you to do your best.

> —*Duke Ellington,*
> *jazz musician*
> *(1899–1974)*

When I've done my best, I get goose bumps.
Nothing is hard when you love what you do.

> —*Marion Jones,*
> *world champion*
> *sprinter and long*
> *jumper (b. 1975)*

Look at a day when you are supremely
satisfied at the end. It's not a day when you
lounge around doing nothing; it's when you've
had everything to do, and you've done it.

> —*Margaret Thatcher,*
> *prime minister, Great Britain*
> *(b. 1925)*

So celebrate what you've accomplished, but raise the bar a little higher each time you succeed.

> —*Mia Hamm,*
> *three-time U.S. Soccer athlete*
> *of the year, 1996 Olympic gold*
> *medalist (b. 1972)*

Cease to be a drudge, seek to be an artist.

> —*Mary McLeod Bethune,*
> *educator (1875–1955)*

Disciplining yourself to do what you know is right and important, although difficult, is the high road to pride, self-esteem, and personal satisfaction.

—*Brian Tracy,*
speaker, writer

Only those who will risk going too far can possibly find out how far one can go.

—*T. S. Eliot,*
poet and critic
(1888–1965)

I don't know the key to success, but the key to failure is trying to please everybody.

—*Bill Cosby,*
actor, comedian
(b. 1937)

Those who truly have the spirit of champions are never wholly happy with an easy win. Half the satisfaction stems from knowing it was the time and the effort you invested that led to your high achievement.

—*Nicole Haislett,*
Olympic swimming
champion (b. 1972)

The world is moving so fast these days that the man who says it can't be done is generally interrupted by someone doing it.

—*Elbert Hubbard,*
writer, editor
(1856–1915)

Always do right. This will gratify some people, and astonish the rest.

—*Mark Twain,*
writer (1835–1910)

A winner's strongest muscle is her heart.

> —*Cassie Campbell,*
> *gold medalist for Team*
> *Canada at 1994 and*
> *1997 World Hockey*
> *Championships*
> *(b. 1973)*

All you can do is your best. You give it everything you have and whether you make it or not, you've done all you can. If you've done that, there's nothing else you can give and you should be proud of yourself.

> —*Joy Fawcett,*
> *member of U.S. women's*
> *national soccer team*
> *(b. 1968)*

You have reached the pinnacle of success as soon as you become uninterested in money, compliments, or publicity.

—*Dr. O. A. Battista*

Change takes guts. It takes imagination. It takes commitment.

—*John Taylor,*
General Motors'
Apex Team

There's a fine line between being conceited and having confidence in yourself. Conceit is thinking you can do it without hard work and practice.

> —*Carol Heiss Jenkins,*
> *Olympic gold medalist*
> *in figure skating*
> *(b. 1940)*

Don't be afraid to give up the good to go for the great.

—*Kenny Rogers,*
country singer
(b. 1938)

It's the struggle that makes you triumphant.

—*Michelle Akers,*
member of U.S. women's
national soccer team
(b. 1966)

Even if you're on the right track, you'll get run over if you just sit there.

—*Will Rogers,*
actor, humorist
(1879–1935)

On the human chessboard, all moves are possible.

—*Miriam Schiff,*
educator

A man of character finds a special attractiveness in difficulty, since it is only by coming to grips with difficulty that he can realize his potentialities.

—*Charles de Gaulle,*
French president and
statesman (1890–1970)

My mother drew a distinction between achievement and success. She said that achievement is the knowledge that you have studied and worked hard and done the best that is in you. Success is being praised by others. That is nice but not as important or satisfying. Always aim for achievement and forget about success.

—*Helen Hayes,*
actress (1900–1993)

Everybody can do something that makes a difference.

—*Todd R. Wagner,*
entrepreneur and
philanthropist, The
Todd R. Wagner
Foundation

When one must, one can.

—*Yiddish proverb*

It's easier to limit yourself, but if you do, you will never reach your full potential.

> —*Chris Witty,*
> *Olympic medalist in*
> *speed skating (b. 1975)*

The best way to keep charged up is to do what's been nagging at you.

> —*Susan Bishop,*
> *founder and president,*
> *Bishop Partners*

The only way to achieve self-esteem is to work hard. People have an obligation to live up to their potential.

> —*Bette Midler,*
> *actress, singer, comedian*
> *(b. 1945)*

We are judged by what we finish, not by what we start.

> —*Anonymous*

We fought hard. We gave it our best. We did
what was right and made a difference.

—*Geraldine A. Ferraro,*
attorney, politician
(b. 1935)

Think creatively, and you can make an impact.

—*Anne McGee-Cooper,*
founder and partner,
Anne McGee-Cooper
and Associates

Risk! Risk anything! Care no more for the opinions of others, for those voices. Do the hardest thing on earth for you. Act for yourself. Face the truth.

—*Katherine Mansfield,*
writer (1888–1923)

The first thing to do in life is to do with
purpose what one proposes to do.

> —*Pablo Casals,*
> *musician, composer,*
> *conductor (1876–1973)*

You may have to fight a battle more than once
to win it.

> —*Margaret Thatcher,*
> *prime minister, Great Britain*
> *(b. 1925)*

You can do anything—but not everything.

> —*David Allen,*
> *personal productivity*
> *thinker*

There is no one else who can ever fill your role in the same way, so it's a good idea to perform it as well as possible.

> —*Humphry Osmond*

Go out into the world, find work that you love, learn from your mistakes, and work hard to make a difference.

> —*Maurice R. Greenberg,*
> *chairman, American*
> *International Group*

Others have done it before me. I can too.

> —*Corporal John Faunce*

Make it a point to do something every day that you don't want to do. This is the golden rule for acquiring the habit of doing your duty without pain.

—*Mark Twain,*
writer (1835–1910)

Confidence doesn't come out of nowhere. It's a result of something . . . hours and days and weeks and years of constant work and dedication.

—*Roger Staubach,*
football player (b. 1942)

Your world is as big as you make it.

—*Georgia Douglas Johnson,*
poet (1866–1966)

The best job goes to the person who can get it done without passing the buck or coming back with excuses.

—*Napoleon Hill,*
speaker, writer
(1883–1970)

People are not the best because they work hard.
They work hard because they are the best.

> —*Bette Midler,*
> *actress, singer, comedian*
> *(b. 1945)*

People may doubt what you say, but they will
believe what you do.

> —*Lewis Cass,*
> *statesman, senator*
> *(1782–1866)*

You can have unbelievable intelligence, you can have connections, you can have opportunities fall out of the sky. But in the end, hard work is the true, enduring characteristic of successful people.

—*Marsha Evans,*
executive director of
Girl Scouts of America

I do not know anyone who has got to the top without hard work. That is the recipe. It will not always get you to the top, but it should get you pretty near.

—*Margaret Thatcher,*
prime minister, Great Britain
(b. 1925)

It is not enough to understand what we ought
to be, unless we know what we are; and we do
not understand what we are, unless we know
what we ought to be.

—*T. S. Eliot,*
poet and critic
(1888–1965)

What the human mind can conceive and
believe, it can accomplish.

> —*David Sarnoff,*
> *broadcast pioneer*
> *(1891–1971)*

I can give you a six-word formula for success:
"Think things through—then follow through."

> —*Edward Rickenbacker,*
> *aviator (1890–1973)*

Above all, challenge yourself. You may well surprise yourself at what strengths you have, what you can accomplish.

—*Cecile M. Springer*

Opportunity follows struggle. It follows effort. It follows hard work. It doesn't come before.

—*Shelby Steele,*
writer (b. 1946)

Behold the turtle. He makes progress only
when he sticks his neck out.

> —*James B. Conant,*
> *chemist, diplomat, educator*
> *(1893–1978)*

When I saw something that needed doing, I did it.

—*Nellie Cashman,*
frontierswoman
(1844–1925)

We should be taught not to wait for inspiration to start a thing. Action always generates inspiration. Inspiration seldom generates action.

—*Frank Tibolt*

The minute you settle for less than you deserve, you get even less than you settled for.

—*Maureen Dowd,*
journalist (b. 1952)

Strategy is better than strength.

—*Hausa legend*

It ain't bragging if you can do it.

—*Dizzy Dean,*
baseball player,
broadcaster
(1911–1974)

No one rises to low expectations.

—*Les Brown,*
motivational speaker,
writer

Never Give Up

You're going to make mistakes in life. It's what you do after the mistakes that counts.

—Brandi Chastain,
World Cup soccer
star (b. 1968)

We may encounter many defeats but we must not be defeated.

—Maya Angelou,
author and poet
(b. 1928)

Ever tried. Ever failed. No matter. Try again.
Fail again. Fail better.

> —*Samuel Beckett,*
> *playwright, novelist*
> *(1906–1989)*

Stumbling is not falling.

> —*Portuguese proverb*

A winner will find a way to win. Winners take bad breaks and use them to drive themselves to be that much better. Quitters take bad breaks and use them as a reason to give up. It's all a matter of pride.

—Nancy Lopez,
golfer, member of the
LPGA Hall of Fame
(b. 1957)

I don't like people who have never fallen or stumbled. Their virtue is lifeless and it isn't of much value. Life hasn't revealed its beauty to them.

> —*Boris Pasternak,*
> *poet, novelist*
> *(1890–1960)*

A mistake is simply another way of doing
things.

> —*Katherine Graham,*
> *publisher of the*
> Washington Post
> *(b. 1917)*

Never confuse a single defeat with a final
defeat.

> —*F. Scott Fitzgerald,*
> *writer (1896–1940)*

Do not let what you cannot do interfere with what you can do.

—*John Wooden,*
college basketball
coach (b. 1910)

In great attempts it is even glorious to fail.

—*Vince Lombardi,*
football coach
(1913–1970)

Don't be afraid of failing. It doesn't matter how many times you fall down. All that matters is how many times you keep getting up.

> —*Marian Wright Edelman,*
> *lawyer, founder of the Children's*
> *Defense Fund (b. 1939)*

Don't give up. Keep going. There is always a chance that you will stumble onto something *terrific*. I have never heard of someone stumbling over something while he was sitting down.

> —*Ann Landers,*
> *advice columnist*
> *(b. 1918)*

The world is one percent good, one percent bad, ninety-eight percent neutral. It can go one way or the other, depending on which side is pushing. This is why what individuals do is important.

—*Hans Habe,*
political activist, writer

Don't let them tell you no. If they say no,
don't believe them. It's all about sticking it out.
If you think you can do it, don't let anyone
laugh at you.

—*Suzyn Waldman,*
New York Yankees
broadcaster

The Wright brothers flew right through the smoke screen of impossibility.

> —*Charles F. Kettering,*
> *engineer, inventor*
> *(1876–1958)*

It takes as much courage to have tried and failed as it does to have tried and succeeded.

> —*Anne Morrow Lindbergh,*
> *writer (1906–2001)*

Oh, we all get run over—once in our lives. But one must pick oneself up again. And behave as if it were nothing.

—*Henrik Ibsen,*
playwright
(1828–1906)

Just go out there and do what you've got to do.

—*Martina Navratilova,*
tennis pro (b. 1956)

How do we break out of the box we're stuck in?
There are lots of reasons why we stay in the box,
but the number-one reason is fear of failure.

> —*Donald Winkler,*
> *chairman and CEO,*
> *Ford Motor Credit Company*

You really don't know what your true potential is until you've pushed yourself beyond your limits. You have to fail a couple of times to really find out how far you can go.

—*Debi Thomas,*
figure skater
(b. 1967)

Never tell a young person that anything cannot be done. God may have been waiting centuries for someone ignorant enough of the impossible to do that very thing.

—*John Andrew Holmes*

If you think you can, you can. And if you think you can't, you're right.

—*Mary Kay Ash,*
founder, Mary Kay Cosmetics

You accomplish victory step by step, not by leaps and bounds.

—*Lyn St. James,*
race-car driver
(b. 1947)

I focus on turning negatives into positives. If you want it and you dream about it, there's nothing that's going to stop you.

> —*Chris Witty,*
> *Olympic medalist*
> *in speed skating*
> *(b. 1975)*

I think luck is the sense to recognize an opportunity and the ability to take advantage of it. Every one has bad breaks, but every one also has opportunities. The man who can smile at his breaks and grab his chances gets on.

—Samuel Goldwyn,
motion-picture producer
(1882–1974)

If you can see [life] as a learning experience,
you can turn any negative into a positive.

—*Neve Campbell,*
actress (b. 1973)

No man ever fails until he fails on the inside.

—*Anonymous*

Effort is only effort when it begins to hurt.

> —*José Ortega y Gasset,*
> *essayist, philosopher*
> *(1883–1955)*

The only way that things change is when
people are willing to take risks.

> —*Stacy Palmer,*
> *editor*

Small acts really can add up to big transformation.

> —*Lynn Ridenour,*
> *vice president of marketing,*
> *GreaterGood.com Inc.*

Failure may be just a step toward your eventual goal.

> —*Georgette Mosbacher,*
> *businesswoman, author*
> *(b. 1947)*

If one takes pride in one's craft, you won't let a good thing die. Risking it through not pushing hard enough is not a humility.

> —*Paul Keating,*
> *Australian statesman*
> *and prime minister*
> *(b. 1944)*

Success is getting up one more time than you fall down.

—*Julie Bowden,*
writer

Being defeated is often a temporary condition. Giving up is what makes it permanent.

—*Marilyn vos Savant,*
columnist, television
talk-show host (b. 1946)

Just because you made a mistake doesn't mean
you *are* a mistake.

> —*Georgette Mosbacher,*
> *businesswoman, author*
> *(b. 1947)*

Perseverance is not a long race; it is many short
races one after another.

—*Walter Elliott,*
priest, writer

When you are looking for obstacles, you can't
find opportunities.

—*J. C. Bell*

Learning
Throughout
Life

I have always grown from my problems and
challenges, from the things that don't work out,
that's when I've really learned.

> —*Carol Burnett,*
> *actress, comedian,*
> *singer (b. 1933)*

Making a wrong decision is understandable.
Refusing to search continually for learning
is not.

—*Philip B. Crosby,*
consultant, author

One's work may be finished someday, but one's education never.

> —*Alexandre Dumas,*
> *novelist, playwright*
> *(1824–1895)*

Lessons are usually where you look for them. You can learn something from anyone.

> —*Brian Koval,*
> *manager, Ryder Carrier*
> *Management*

What matters most is that we learn from living.

> —*Doris Lessing,*
> *novelist, playwright*
> *(b. 1919)*

Are you green and growing, or ripe and rotten?

> —*Ray Kroc,*
> *founder, McDonald's*
> *(1902–1984)*

Growth is the only evidence of life.

> —*Cardinal John Henry Newman,*
> *prelate and theologian*
> *(1801–1890)*

Life is now in session. Are you present?

> —*B. Copeland*

There's always room for improvement, you
know—it's the biggest room in the house.

>—*Louise Heath Leber,*
> New York Post's
> *Mother of the Year, 1961*

Who is not satisfied with himself will grow; who is not so sure of his own correctness will learn many things.

—*Palestinian proverb*

Knowledge is the eye of desire and can become the pilot of the soul.

—*Will Durant,*
historian
(1885–1981)

It is not the answer that enlightens, but the question.

—Eugène Ionesco,
dramatist
(1912–1994)

No man can dream character into himself; he must hammer and forge himself into a man.

—John Wanamaker,
merchant
(1838–1922)

Discovery consists in seeing what everybody
has seen and thinking what nobody has
thought.

> —*Albert Szent-Györgyi,*
> *Nobel laureate in medicine*
> *(1893–1986)*

Knowledge is not a loose-leaf notebook of facts. Above all, it is a responsibility for the integrity of what we are, primarily of what we are as ethical creatures.

—*Jacob Bronowski,*
scientist, writer, broadcaster
(1908–1974)

What you dislike in another take care to correct in yourself.

> —*Thomas Sprat,*
> *historian (1635–1713)*

Of all our human resources, the most precious is the desire to improve.

> —*Anonymous*

Only when your consciousness is totally
focused on the moment you are in can you
receive whatever gift, lesson, or delight that
moment has to offer.

—*Barbara De Angelis,*
author, television
personality

If one is too lazy to think, too vain to do a thing badly, too cowardly to admit it, one will never attain wisdom.

> —*Cyril Connolly,*
> *writer, journalist*
> *(1903–1974)*

To live is to be slowly born.

> —*Antoine de Saint-Exupéry,*
> *aviator, writer*
> *(1900–1944)*

People never improve unless they look to some standard or example higher or better than themselves.

—*Tryon Edwards*
(1809–1894)

It is best to learn as we go, not go as we have learned.

—*Leslie Jeanne Sahler*

The first step to knowledge is to know that we are ignorant.

—*Lord David Cecil,*
biographer (1902–1986)

We don't remain good if we don't always strive to become better.

—*Gottfried Keller,*
writer (1819–1890)

Certainly it is almost more important how a person takes his fate than what it is.

—*Wilhelm von Humboldt,*
diplomat and philologist
(1767–1835)

The brighter you are, the more you have to learn.

> —*Don Herold,*
> *author, humorist*
> *(1889–1966)*

Knowledge is the only instrument of production that is not subject to diminishing returns.

> —*J. M. Clark*

If the shoe fits, you're not allowing for growth.

—*Robert N. Coons*

When you're through learning, you're through.

—*Vernon Law,*
baseball player
(b. 1930)

Real education means to inspire people to live more abundantly, to learn to begin with life as they find it and make it better.

—*Carter G. Woodson,*
historian, educator
(1875–1950)

It's what you learn after you know it all that counts.

—*John Wooden,*
college basketball
coach (b. 1910)

Standards of
Excellence

I won't accept anything less than the best a player's capable of doing . . . and he has the right to expect the best that I can do for him and the team!

—*Lou Holtz,*
football coach
(b. 1937)

If you do things well, do them better. Be daring, be first, be different, be just.

—*Anita Roddick,*
founder, The Body Shop

The only sin is mediocrity.

> —*Martha Graham,*
> *founder, Martha Graham*
> *Dance Company*
> *(1894–1991)*

Just do what you do best.

> —*Red Auerbach,*
> *basketball coach*
> *(b. 1917)*

Don't bunt. Aim out of the ballpark. Aim for the company of immortals.

>*—David Ogilvy,*
>*cofounder, Ogilvy &*
>*Mather Advertising*
>*(1911–1999)*

The dedicated life is the life worth living. You must give with your whole heart.

>*—Annie Dillard,*
>*writer (b. 1945)*

Class is an aura of confidence that is being sure without being cocky. Class has nothing to do with money. Class never runs scared. It is self-discipline and self-knowledge. It's the sure-footedness that comes with having proved you can meet life.

—*Ann Landers,*
   advice columnist
   (b. 1918)

My attitude is never to be satisfied, never enough, never.

>   —*Bela Karolyi,*
>   *Olympics gymnastic*
>   *coach (b. 1942)*

The secret of joy in work is contained in one word—excellence. To know how to do something well is to enjoy it.

>   —*Pearl S. Buck,*
>   *writer (1892–1973)*

I can't imagine a person becoming a success
who doesn't give this game of life everything
he's got.

> —*Walter Cronkite,*
> *news broadcaster*
> *(b. 1916)*

I had a boss at Citibank who used to say, "I never want to be the first. I just want to be the best." And I agree with that.

> —*Wanda Rapaczynksi,*
> *president and CEO of*
> *Agora, media company*
> *in Poland (b. 1947)*

I've always had something to shoot for each
year: to jump one inch further.

—Jackie Joyner-Kersee,
Olympic gold medalist in
track and field (b. 1962)

With confidence, you can reach truly amazing
heights; without confidence, even the simplest
accomplishments are beyond your grasp.

—Jim Loehr,
sports psychologist

Where I was born and where and how I have lived is unimportant. It is what I have done with where I have been that should be of interest.

—*Georgia O'Keeffe,*
artist (1887–1986)

The definition of happiness: . . . the full use of your powers along lines of excellence.

—*John F. Kennedy,*
president (1917–1963)

Winning doesn't always mean being first.
Winning means you're doing better than you've
ever done before.

> —*Bonnie Blair,*
> *Olympic gold medalist*
> *in speed skating*
> *(b. 1964)*

It's a fine thing to rise above pride, but you must have pride in order to do so.

> —*Georges Bernanos,*
> *writer (1888–1948)*

Take something ordinary and elevate it to something extraordinary.

> —*Samuel Mockbee,*
> *professor of architecture,*
> *Auburn University,*
> *Alabama (b. 1944)*

In order to deal with the chaos that exists in the world today, you need some grounding. That grounding best comes from knowing who you are.

—Michael Ray,
professor, Stanford Graduate
School of Business

I'd rather do something interesting, solve an interesting problem, than do something boring and get rich.

—Louis Monier,
Internet entrepreneur

We are here to add what we can to life, not to get what we can from it.

—William Osler,
physician
(1849–1919)

I hope that my achievements in life shall be these—that I will have fought for what was right and fair, that I will have risked for that which mattered, and that I will have given help to those who were in need, that I will have left the earth a better place for what I've done and who I've been.

—*C. Hoppe*

To remain whole, be twisted!
To become straight, let yourself be bent.
To become full, be hollow.
Be tattered, that you may be renewed.

> —*Lao-tzu,*
> *Chinese philosopher*
> *(sixth century B.C.)*

I've never valued my worth in terms of how big my kingdom is. I've valued it based on the impact that I'm having.

> —*Janiece Webb,*
>   *senior vice president,*
>   *Motorola*

Let us endeavor so to live that when we come to die even the undertaker will be sorry.

> —*Mark Twain,*
>   *writer (1835–1910)*

A man's reputation is the opinion people have of him; his character is what he really is.

—*Jack Miner,*
conservationist
(1865–1944)

It's important to let people know what you stand for. It's equally important that they know what you won't stand for.

—*B. Bader*

Be True
to Yourself

You have to believe in yourself. The ones who
believe in themselves the most are the ones
who win.

> —*Florence Griffith-Joyner,*
> *winner of three gold medals*
> *at the 1988 Olympics*
> *(1959–1998)*

You have to count on living every single day in
a way you believe will make you feel good about
your life—so that if it were over tomorrow,
you'd be content with yourself.

—Jane Seymour,
actress (b. 1951)

You really have to look inside yourself and find your own inner strength, and say, "I'm proud of what I am and who I am, and I'm just going to be myself."

—*Mariah Carey,*
singer, songwriter
(b. 1970)

So many of us define ourselves by what we have, what we wear, what kind of house we live in and what kind of car we drive. . . . If you think of yourself as the woman in the Cartier watch and the Hermès scarf, a house fire will destroy not only your possessions but your self.

—*Linda Henley*

Trust yourself. Create the kind of self that you will be happy to live with all your life. Make the most of yourself by fanning the tiny, inner sparks of possibility into flames of achievement.

—*Foster C. McClellan*

Follow your instincts. That's where true wisdom manifests itself.

> —*Oprah Winfrey,*
> *television talk-show*
> *host, actress (b. 1954)*

We define ourselves by the best that is in us, not the worst that has been done to us.

> —*Edward Lewis,*
> *cofounder and CEO,*
> Essence

What lies ahead of you and what lies behind you is nothing compared to what lies within you.

> —*Mohandas K. Gandhi,*
> *leader of the Indian*
> *movement for independence*
> *(1869–1948)*

Emotional competence is the single most
important personal quality that each of us
must develop and access to experience a
breakthrough.

> —*Doug Lennick,*
> *American Express*
> *Brokerage*

I believed I could do anything I could think of. So the challenge was always to keep thinking— to get to where I wanted to be and then to think of somewhere else to go.

—*Bette Midler,*
actress, singer, comedian
(b. 1945)

I was always looking outside myself for strength and confidence but it comes from within. It was there all the time.

—*Anna Freud,*
psychoanalyst
(1895–1982)

Knowing who you are begins in the mind.

—*Bebe Moore Campbell,*
author (b. 1950)

Don't just fit in with the crowd and be normal,
try to be extraordinary.

—*Kerri Strug,*
winner of Olympic gold
medal in gymnastics
(b. 1977)

You've got to find something in your efforts that has meaning to you, and only you can define that. Once you define it, you are going to be much more at peace with what you are doing.

—*Silken Laumann,*
Canadian Olympic medalist
in rowing (b. 1964)

Who I am is the best I can be.

> —*Leontyne Price,*
> *opera singer*
> *(b. 1927)*

You have got to discover you, what you do, and trust it.

> —*Barbra Streisand,*
> *actress, singer, film*
> *producer (b. 1942)*

When you have self-respect you have enough, and when you have enough, you have self-respect.

—*Gail Sheehy,*
writer (b. 1937)

Originality does not consist in saying what no one has ever said before, but in saying exactly what you think yourself.

—*James Stephens,*
writer (1882–1950)

Ultimately, it's not a matter of which style works better than the other. It all comes down to which style works best for you.

—*Simon Walker,*
managing director,
Challenge Business

We are not permitted to choose the frame of our destiny. But what we put into it is ours.

> —*Dag Hammarskjöld,*
> *Swedish statesman,*
> *secretary-general of*
> *the UN (1905–1961)*

There is an applause superior to that of the multitude—one's own.

> —*Elizabeth Elton Smith*

There is no paycheck that can equal the feeling of contentment that comes from being the person you are meant to be.

—*Oprah Winfrey,*
television talk-show
host, actress (b. 1954)

I realized that it's okay to take risks and make choices based on your heart as opposed to your pocketbook or anybody else's opinion.

—*Melina Kanakaredes,*
actress (b. 1967)

Your sole contribution to the sum of things is
yourself.

> —*Frank Crane,*
> *essayist*

We possess nothing in the world—except the
power to say "I."

> —*Simone Weil,*
> *philosopher, mystic,*
> *writer (1909–1943)*

The willingness to accept responsibility for one's own life is the source from which self-respect springs.

—*Joan Didion,*
writer (b. 1934)

You have to make taking care of yourself a
priority.

> *—Christina Maslach,*
> *professor of psychology,*
> *University of California,*
> *Berkeley*

You are what you are when nobody is looking.

> *—Abigail Van Buren,*
> *advice columnist*
> *(b. 1918)*

Whatever you want in life, others are going to want it too. Believe in yourself enough to accept the idea that you have an equal right to it.

—Diane Sawyer,
broadcast journalist
(b. 1945)

Our lives teach us who we are.

—Salman Rushdie,
author (b. 1947)

192

Our achievements speak for themselves. What we have to keep track of are our failures, discouragements, and doubts. We tend to forget the past difficulties, the many false starts, and the painful groping.

—*Eric Hoffer,*
writer, philosopher
(1902–1983)

If you wish to achieve worthwhile things in your personal and career life, you must become a worthwhile person in your own self-development.

—*Brian Tracy,*
speaker, writer

I had learned how to nurture myself, so besides
hearing a critical voice, I had another voice
inside me that said, I believe in you. Whatever
you do is fine.

—*Laurel King*

It ain't nothing to find no starting place in the world. You just start from where you find yourself.

—*August Wilson,*
playwright (b. 1945)

There is always one true inner voice. Trust it.

—*Gloria Steinem,*
writer, feminist
(b. 1934)

When you are at ease with yourself, you are
able to utilize all your gifts and fulfill your
purpose in life. You are able to give to others
unselfishly and receive from them, knowing
you are worthy.

—*Oprah Winfrey,*
television talk-show
host, actress (b. 1954)

The more you listen to the voice within you,
the better you will hear what is sounding
outside.

> —*Dag Hammarskjöld,*
> *Swedish statesman,*
> *secretary-general of*
> *the UN (1905–1961)*

Personal power, which is derived from our ability to act in the interest of ourselves and others, is developed from our ability to first clearly see and understand ourselves.

—*Jill Janov*

People who succeed speak well of themselves
to themselves.

> —*Laurie Beth Jones,*
> *motivational speaker,*
> *writer*

Your worth consists in what you are and not in
what you have; what you are will show in what
you do.

> —*Thomas Davidson,*
> *clergyman*

All psychological problems, from the slightest neurosis to the deepest psychosis, are merely symptoms of the frustration of the fundamental need for a sense of personal worth. Self-esteem is the basic element in the health of any human personality.

—*Dr. William Glasser,*
founder of William
Glasser Institute

If you have no confidence in self you are twice defeated in the race of life. With confidence you have won even before you have started.

—*Marcus Garvey,*
Jamaican black-
nationalist leader
(1887–1940)

You've got to take the initiative and play your game. In a decisive set, confidence is the difference.

—*Chris Evert,*
tennis pro
(b. 1954)

A human being's first responsibility is to shake hands with himself.

—*Henry Winkler,*
actor (b. 1945)

Be yourself. No one can ever tell you you're doing it wrong.

> —*James Leo Herlihy,*
> *actor, playwright, novelist,*
> *teacher (1927–1993)*

You have to know that your real home is within.

> —*Quincy Jones,*
> *musician, composer*
> *(b. 1933)*

I know that no one can really stop me but myself and that really no one can help me but myself.

—*Peter Nivio Zarlenga*

To have that sense of one's intrinsic worth
which constitutes self-respect is potentially to
have everything.

—*Joan Didion,*
writer (b. 1934)

People who take time to be alone usually have depth, originality, and quiet reserve.

—*John Miller*

We don't know who we are until we see what we can do.

—*Martha Grimes,*
writer

The most important things ever said to us are said by our inner selves.

> —*Adelaide Bry,*
> *writer (b. 1920)*